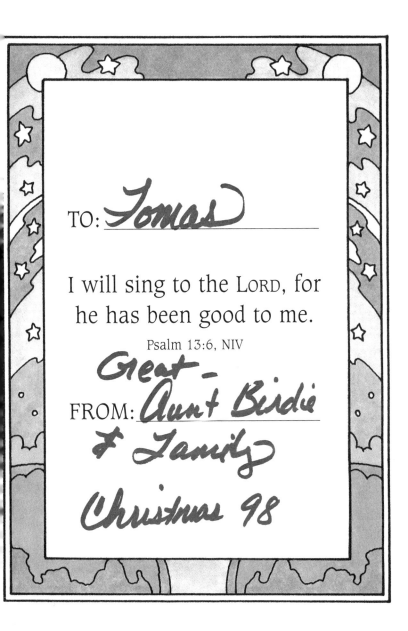

TO: _Tomas_

I will sing to the LORD, for
he has been good to me.

Psalm 13:6, NIV

FROM: _Great-_
Aunt Birdie
& Family

Christmas 98

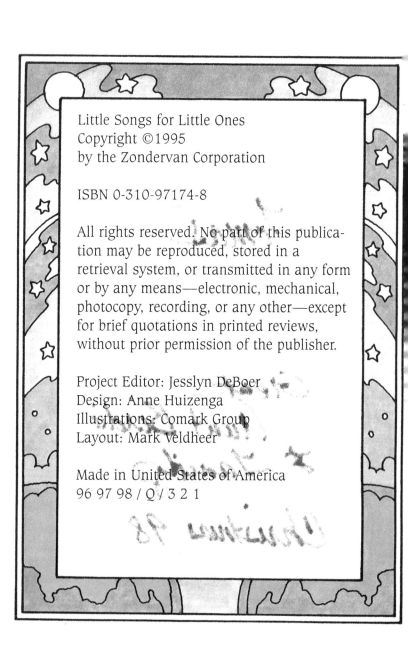

Little Songs for Little Ones
Copyright ©1995
by the Zondervan Corporation

ISBN 0-310-97174-8

Project Editor: Jesslyn DeBoer
Design: Anne Huizenga
Illustrations: Comark Group
Layout: Mark Veldheer

Made in United States of America
96 97 98 / Q / 3 2 1

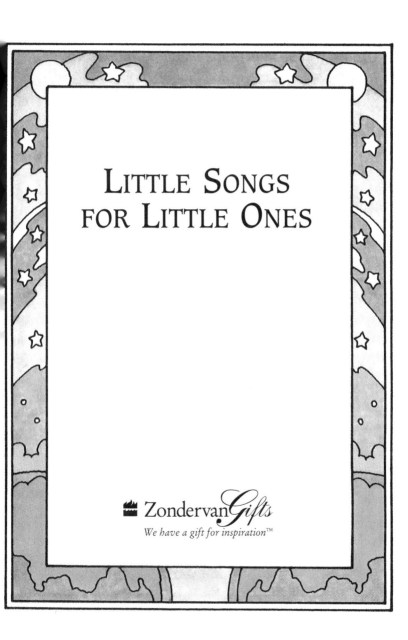

LITTLE SONGS
FOR LITTLE ONES

Zondervan*Gifts*

We have a gift for inspiration™

To Tomas
who everyone
loves,
Great Aunt
Birdie
& Family

Christmas 98

Fill your heart with God's joy and sing praise to him with these little songs:

*He's Got the Whole World
in His Hands
The B-I-B-L-E
Oh, Be Careful
Away in a Manger
Jesus Loves Me
I Will Make You Fishers of Men
Zacchaeus
The Wise Man and
the Foolish Man
Onward, Christian Soldiers
This Little Light of Mine
Jesus Loves the Little Children
The Lord's My Shepherd*

HE'S GOT THE WHOLE WORLD IN HIS HANDS

He's got the whole
world in his hands.
He's got the whole
world in his hands.

He's got the whole
world in his hands.
He's got the whole
world in his hands.

He's got the wind
and the rain
in his hands.
(Sing 3 times)

He's got the whole
world in his hands.

He's got the little
tiny baby
in his hands.
(Sing 3 times)

He's got the whole
world in his hands.

He's got
everybody here
in his hands.
(Sing 3 times)

He's got the whole
world in his hands.

THE B-I-B-L-E

The B-I-B-L-E

Yes, that's the book
for me!

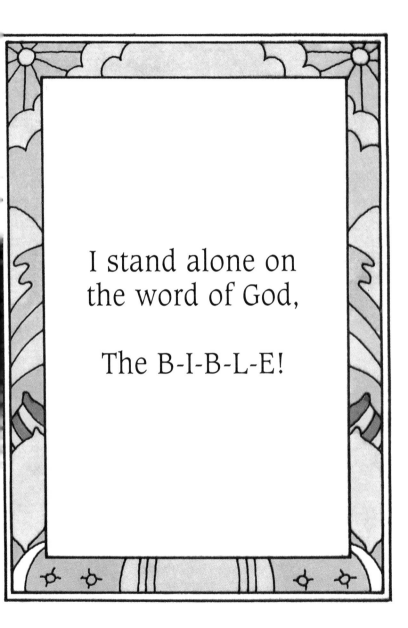

I stand alone on the word of God,

The B-I-B-L-E!

OH, BE CAREFUL

Oh, be careful
little hands
what you do.

Oh, be careful
little hands
what you do.

For the Father
up above
is looking down
in love,
So be careful
little hands
what you do.

Oh, be careful
little tongue what
you say.

Oh, be careful
little tongue what
you say.

For the Father
up above
is looking down
in love,
So be careful
little tongue
what you say.

AWAY IN
A MANGER

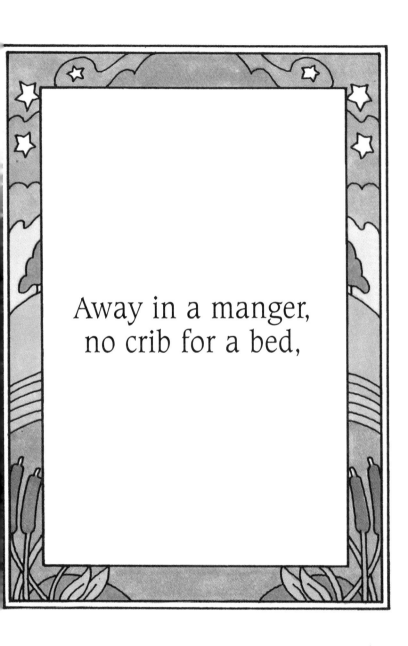

Away in a manger,
no crib for a bed,

the little Lord Jesus
laid down his
sweet head;

the stars in the
sky looked down
where he lay;

the little Lord Jesus
asleep on the hay.

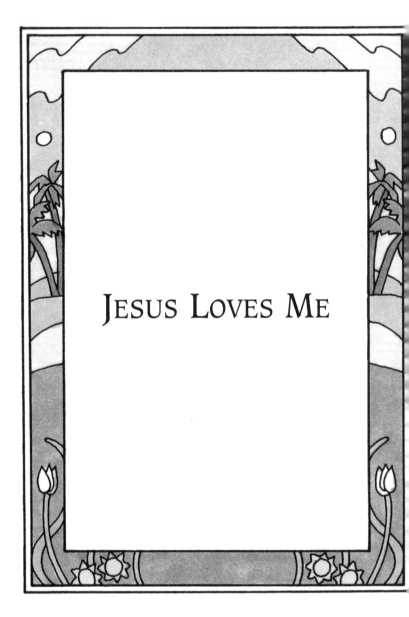

JESUS LOVES ME

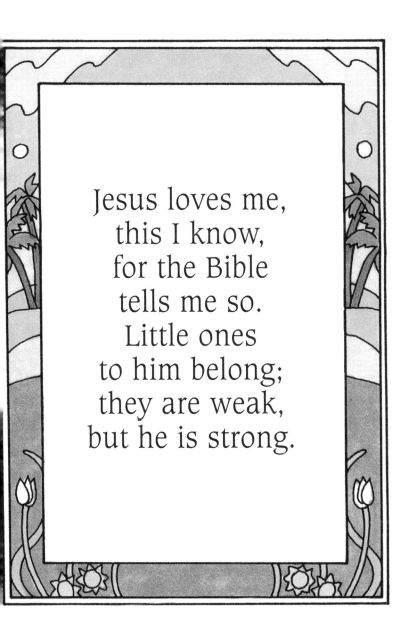

Jesus loves me,
this I know,
for the Bible
tells me so.
Little ones
to him belong;
they are weak,
but he is strong.

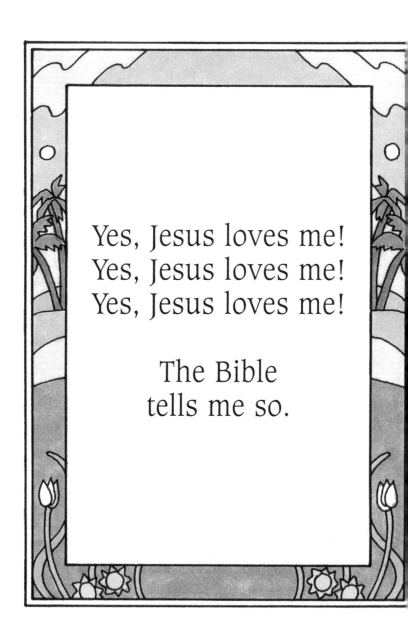

Yes, Jesus loves me!
Yes, Jesus loves me!
Yes, Jesus loves me!

The Bible
tells me so.

Jesus loves me–
he who died
heaven's gate
to open wide.
He will wash
away my sin,
let his little
child come in.

Yes, Jesus loves me!
Yes, Jesus loves me!
Yes, Jesus loves me!

The Bible
tells me so.

I Will Make You Fishers of Men

If you follow me,
if you follow me,
I will make you
fishers of men,
if you follow me.

Hear Christ calling,
"Come unto me.
Come unto me.
Come unto me."

Hear Christ calling,
"Come unto me.
I will give you rest."

"I will give you rest.
I will give you rest."
Hear Christ calling,
"Come unto me.
I will give you rest."

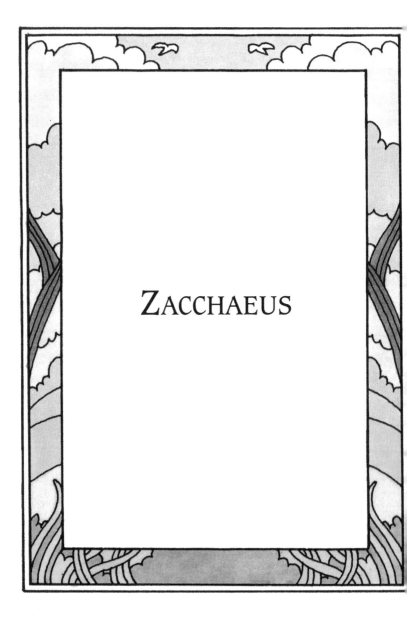

ZACCHAEUS

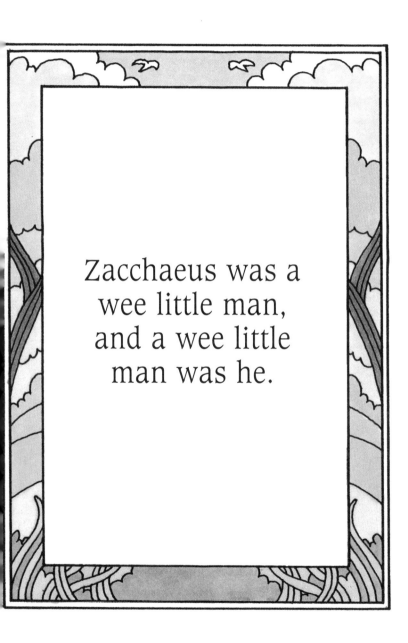

Zacchaeus was a
wee little man,
and a wee little
man was he.

He climbed up in a
Sycamore tree
For the Lord he
wanted to see;
And as the Savior
passed that way,
He looked up
in the tree,

And He said,
"Zacchaeus,
you come down,
For I'm going to your
house today,

For I'm going to your house today."

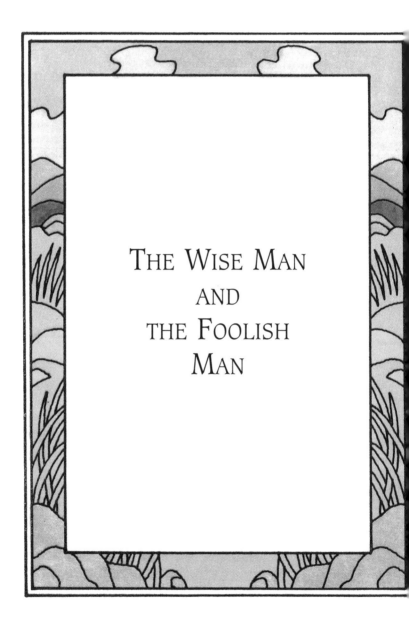

THE WISE MAN
AND
THE FOOLISH
MAN

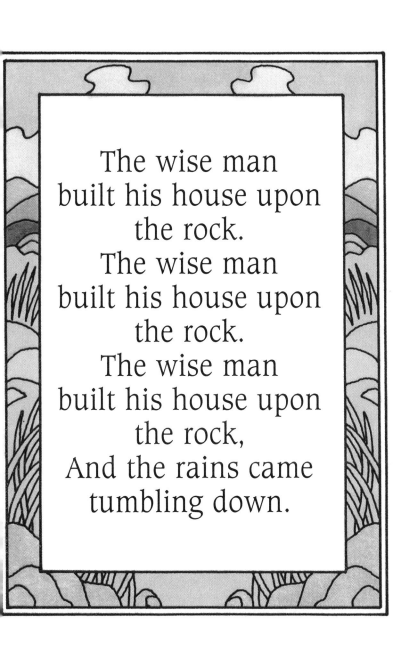

The wise man
built his house upon
the rock.
The wise man
built his house upon
the rock.
The wise man
built his house upon
the rock,
And the rains came
tumbling down.

The rains came
down and the floods
came up.
The rains came
down and the floods
came up.
The rains came
down and the floods
came up,
And the house on
the rocks stood firm.

The foolish man
built his house upon
the sand.
The foolish man
built his house upon
the sand.
The foolish man
built his house upon
the sand,
And the rains came
tumbling down.

The rains came
down and the floods
came up.
The rains came
down and the floods
came up.
The rains came
down and the floods
came up,
And the house on
the sand went
SMASH!

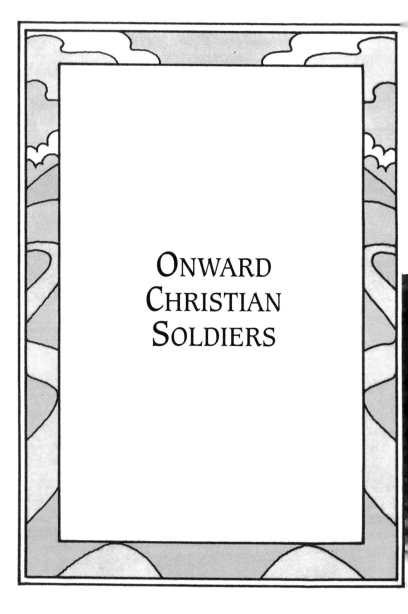

ONWARD
CHRISTIAN
SOLDIERS

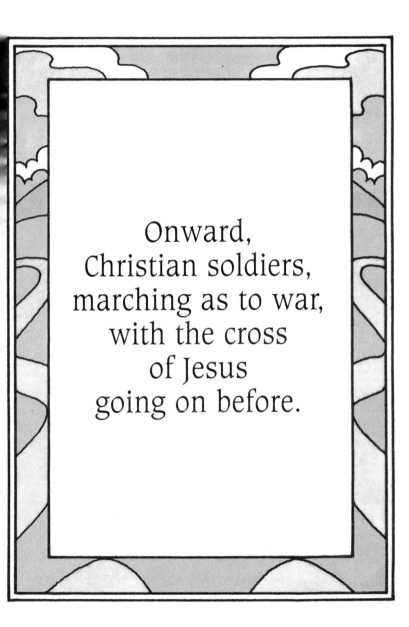

Onward,
Christian soldiers,
marching as to war,
with the cross
of Jesus
going on before.

Christ
the royal master,
leads against the foe;
forward into battle
see his banners go!

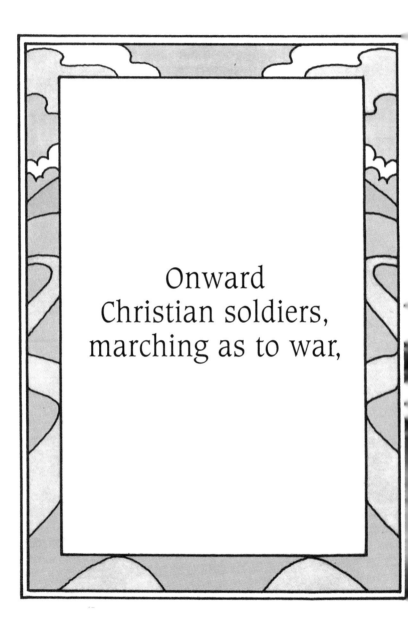

Onward
Christian soldiers,
marching as to war,

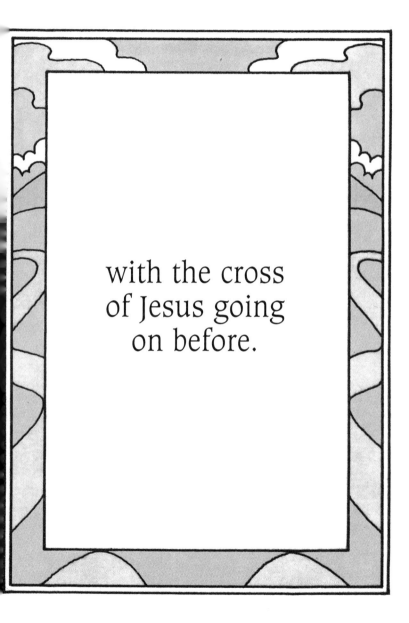

with the cross
of Jesus going
on before.

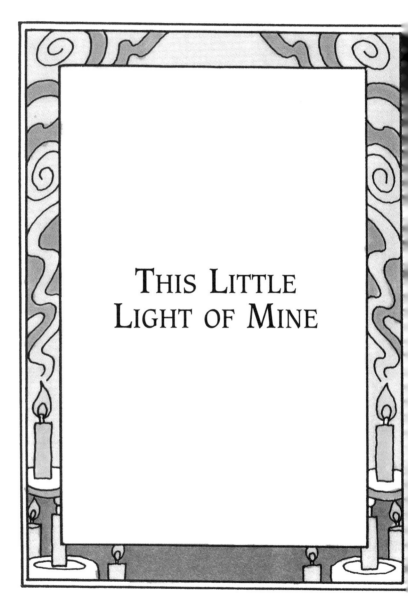

THIS LITTLE
LIGHT OF MINE

This little light
of mine,
I'm gonna let
it shine.
This little light
of mine,
I'm gonna let
it shine.
Let it shine.
Let it shine.
Let it shine.

Don't let Satan
blow it out,
I'm gonna let
it shine.
Don't let Satan
blow it out,
I'm gonna let
it shine.

Let it shine.
Let it shine.
Let it shine.

Jesus Loves the Little Children

Jesus loves
the little children,

All the children
of the world.

Red and yellow,
black and white,
They are precious
in his sight,

Jesus loves
the little children
of the world.

THE LORD'S MY SHEPHERD

The Lord's
my shepherd;
I'll not want.

He makes me
down to lie
in pastures green;

He leadeth me
the quiet waters by.